SUPPLY AND DEMAND

DAY TRADING

Using Price Momentum and Volume

Abraham Robert. C

In order to say thank you for purchasing this book, we offer two of our premium video course to you as a token of appreciation

Find the Link to the bonus video courses at the end of the book

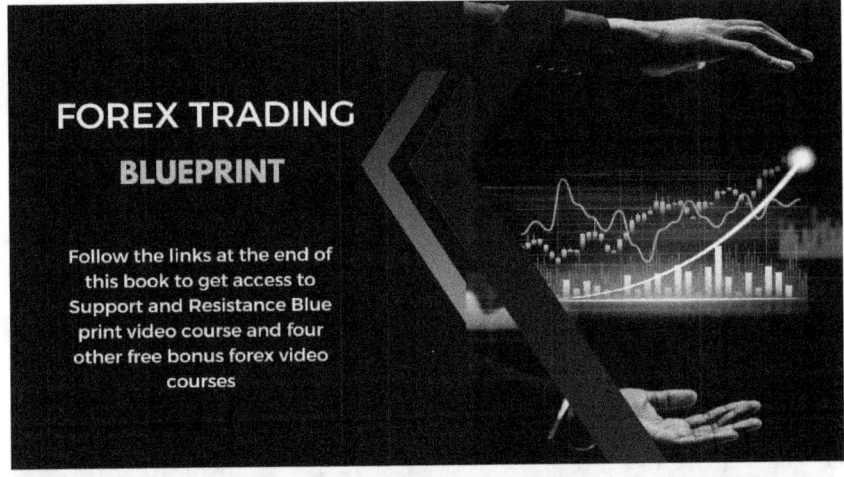

TABLE OF CONTENT

CHAPTER 1

Overview of Demand and Supply

The idea of supply and demand is ageless. It is and always will be the most straightforward and atomic explanation for price fluctuations. This is so that the transaction of trading a product for cash may take place, as the market is the meeting point for buyers and sellers.

Finding Support and demand zones on charts will be fairly easy if you grasp the idea of supply and demand. Even though this is a retrospective observation, it will provide us with a decent indication of where to search for our trades going forward. It is crucial to realize that the analysis and definition of historical zones forms the foundation of the supply and demand theory of for trading. These zones tell us where future price movements should be expected.

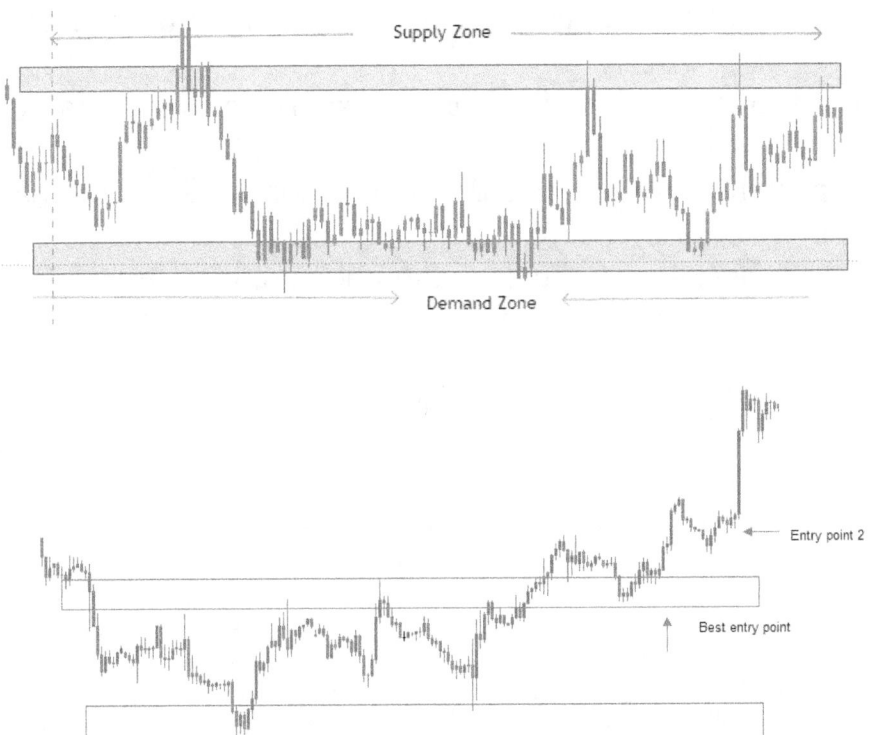

A fundamental understanding of supply and demand is essential for effective trading of foreign exchange.

It is the primary factor influencing price variations of all traded assets, including forex currency pairings.

In actuality, supply and demand trading is the main area of concentration for many experienced traders who specialize in the naked price action trading approach. And there's a valid explanation behind that.

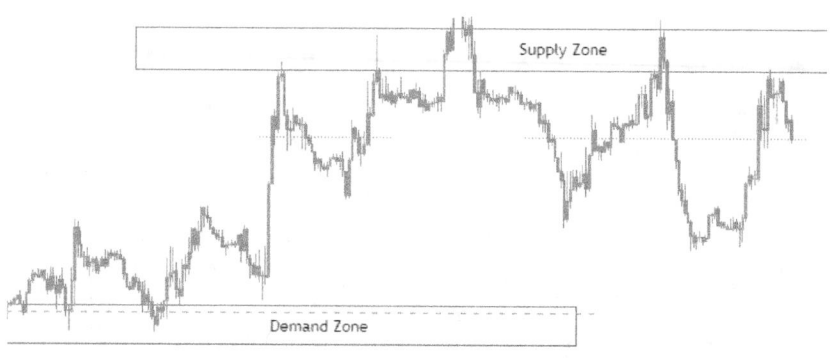

This refers to regions on a chart where an imbalance between buyers and sellers is likely to cause a change in the direction of a currency pair's price movement.

When there is a noticeable rise in buying or selling pressure, these zones appear on the chart. Traders frequently search for trading opportunities when the price of a financial asset hits these levels once more. They do this with the idea that the price will either reverse or continue in the same direction.

Let's go back to the fundamentals of forex trading first and establish supply and demand. The law of supply and demand states that when there is a strong demand—that is, when there are more buyers than sellers for a certain currency pair, the price will increase. On the other hand, if one currency pair is in more supply than the other and there are more sellers than buyers, the price of that currency pair will decrease.

One of the most fundamental trading ideas that you will learn from any trade coaching program is supply and demand.

However, it is not the only thing. Every marketable asset's price has to eventually reach equilibrium. Zones of supply and demand are produced by this. Prices halt as they strike a balance between buyers and sellers, even in a trending market. In forex trading, such is the idea of supply and demand zones. Price action traders employ this technique to identify trading zones by applying the economic principle of supply and demand.

These days, in the world of forex trading, variables including political developments, economic policies, and market mood may have a big influence on the supply and demand of a currency.

In the event that the United States Federal Reserve raises interest rates, for example, it is quite probable that investors will purchase American bonds, fixed-income investments, and other deposits that yield high yearly income, increasing demand for the US currency relative to other currencies.

You'll discover how to identify supply and demand zones with ease and incorporate them into your trading strategy with the help of this book. Thus, remember to read through to the end!

CHAPTER 2

Supply Zone

On a price chart, a supply zone is a region with strong selling power that can cause a price drop or reversal of an upward trend.

If the price has repeatedly failed to break through a level, suggesting strong selling pressure, you can find supply zones.

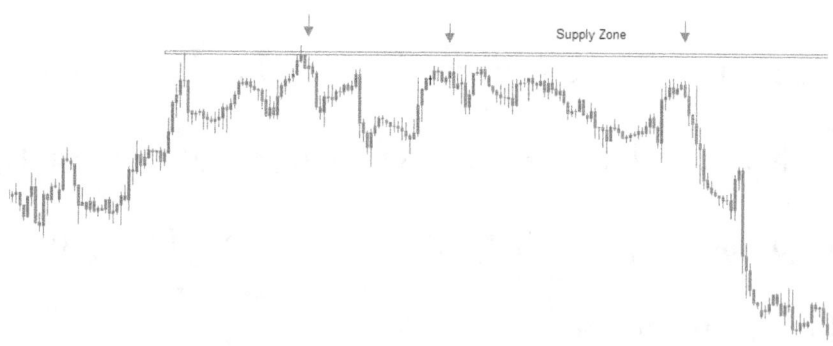

A supply zone, like a demand zone, is an area that market players anticipate acting as a level of resistance.

In a price chart, the supply zone, often referred to as the distribution zone, is where traders try to sell the market. The zone generally appears after a substantial price increase, giving big institutions and individual traders the chance to sell high.

The zone has the biggest selling interest or potential since it is present above the current price level.

When the exchange rate of a currency pair rises to a certain level and then encounters resistance, it either reverses to the downside or consolidates, creating a supply zone. A supply zone provides more resistance to future increases in the exchange rate if it experiences more downward reversals.

CHAPTER 3

Demand Zone

A demand zone is a region where traders often purchase at a certain price. This is the region where the most purchasing interest or possibility is found, below the current price. There are usually plenty of buyers accessible with purchase orders at that level in a recognized demand

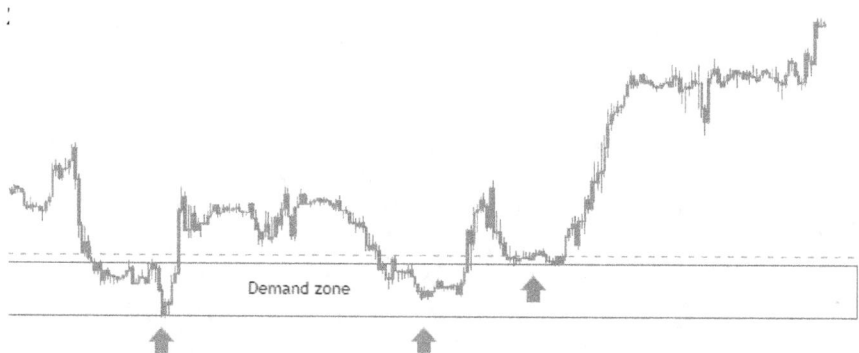

Demand zone

The price range in the market where there is a strong degree of demand and buyers are willing to buy at various points is known as the demand zone. The demand zone, which offers the greatest purchasing opportunity, is found below the current price level.

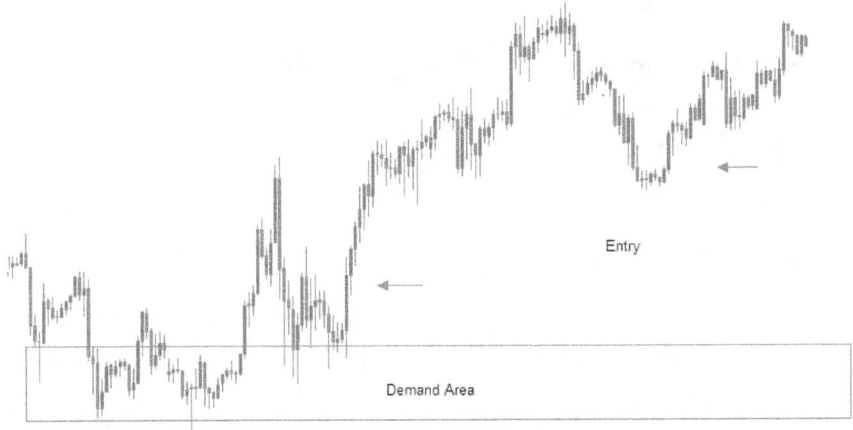

As a trader, you should be aware that accumulation occurs in a purchasing zone; in this instance, the demand zone is the location of bullish trends.

CHAPTER 4

Types of Supply and Demand Patterns

U nderstanding the patterns that play a role in supply and demand zones is crucial. The supply and demand zones exhibit reversal and continuation patterns, just like conventional price pattern analysis.

Reversal Patterns

These patterns essentially describe circumstances in which the dominant price trend flips, moving from up to down or from down to up. In order to better comprehend these patterns, let's look at two examples of structures:

Drop Base Rally: In this pattern, the price descends, hangs out about a broad price level for a while to form a base structure, and then makes a last upward rally.

Drop base rally

Rally Base Drop: In this pattern, the price makes an upward rally, forms a base structure, and then makes a large downward fall. Primary Types of Zones of Supply and Demand

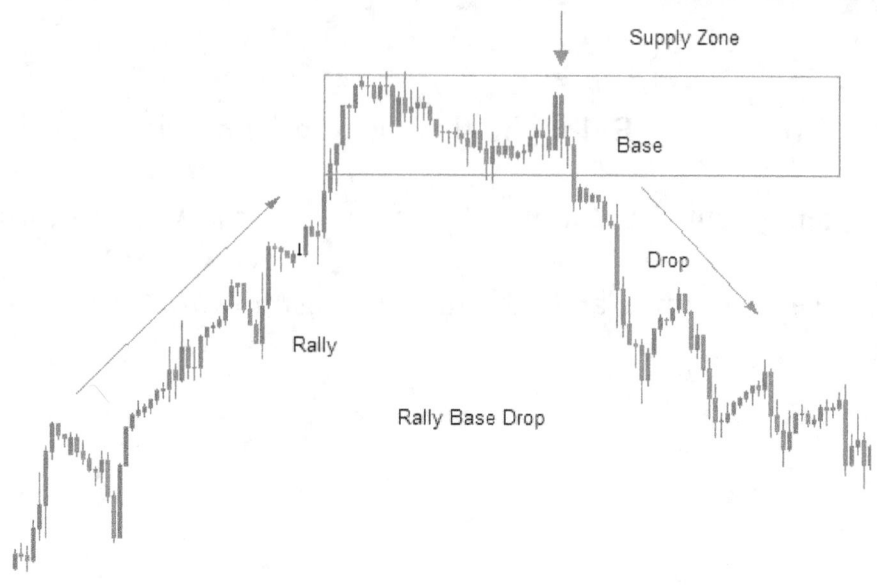

Understanding the patterns that play a role in supply and demand zones is crucial. The supply and demand zones exhibit reversal and continuation patterns, just like conventional price pattern analysis.

Following the rally-base-drop pattern, you can see the price in the supply zone rising, stalling for a while, and then sharply falling. The manner the price exits the base structure is the important thing to observe.

The length of the candles that depict the decline indicates how severe the supply-demand mismatch was at that particular price point.

It is evident from the demand zone structures that the price will drop sharply, form a base, and then rise in accordance with the drop-base-rally structure.

Continuation Patterns

When a price trend persists in following the direction of the dominant general price trend, either upward or downward, this is referred to as a continuation pattern. Since price typically breaks through these formations, these patterns are typically weak. Let's examine the two varieties of continuation patterns to have a better understanding of them:

Drop-Base-Drop: In this pattern, the price declines, takes a little break to form a base, and then keeps falling sharply.

Rally-Base-Rally: In this pattern, the price rises, takes a little break to form a base, and then continues rising.

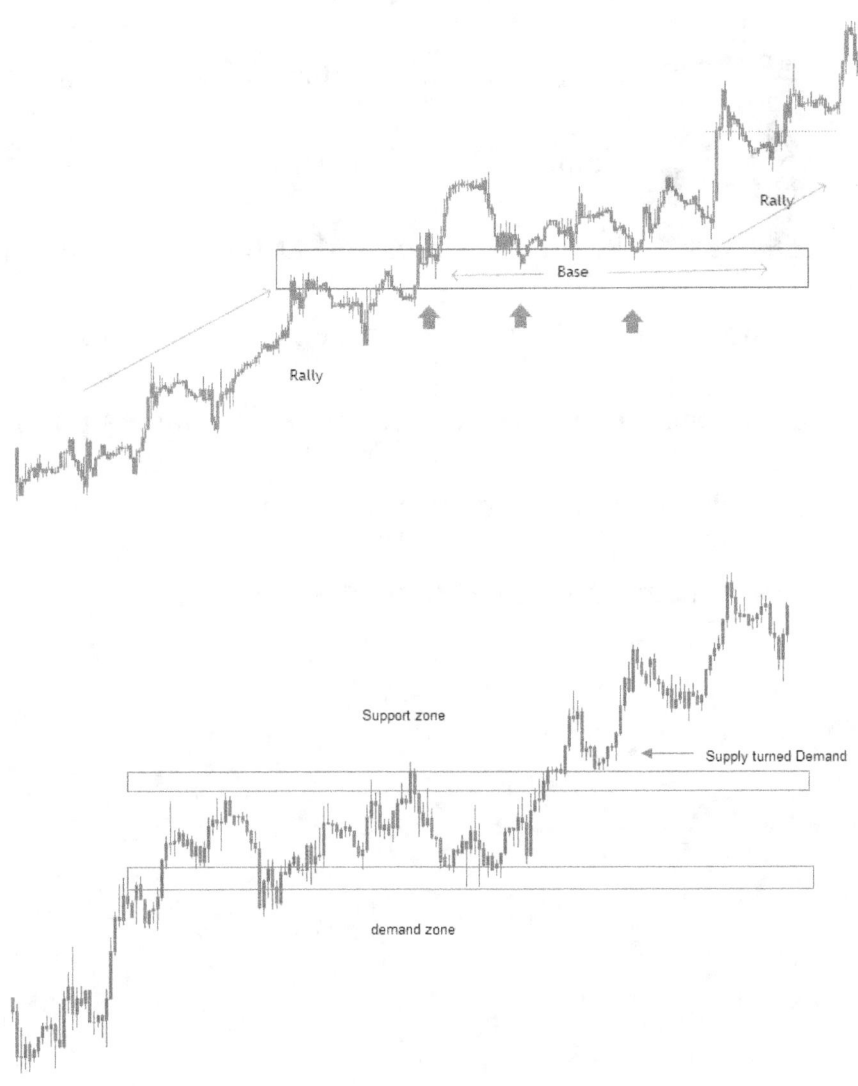

CHAPTER 5

Day Trading Supply and Demand

Buying and selling currencies within a single trading day is known as forex day trading. Positions are closed at the end of each day and new ones are opened the next day. To profit from minute changes in the market, forex day traders purchase and sell a number of currency pairings in the same day, or even many times in a single day.

15 mins entry candle

Demand zone

Day trading, also known as intra-day trading, is not something that is suitable for part-timers since it requires a certain attitude, time, attention, and concentration. It entails making snap judgements and carrying out several deals for marginal profits each time. It is typically perceived as the antithesis of most investing methods, which aim to generate long-term profits from price changes.

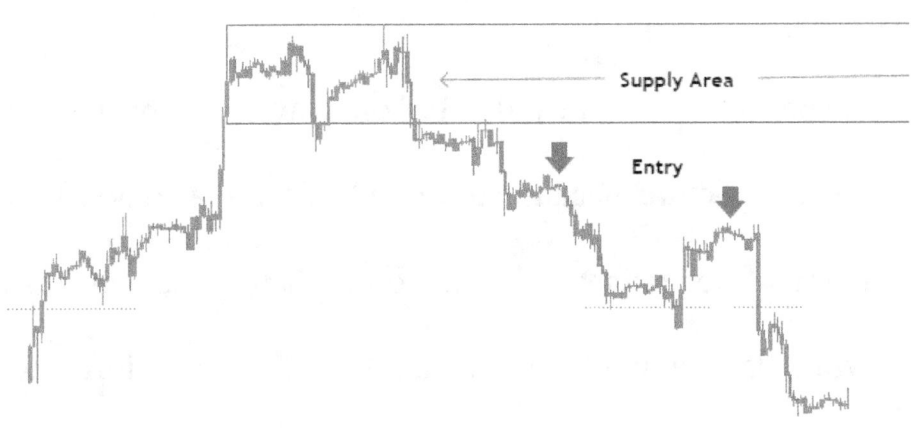

Before you begin day trading forex, or any other market, there are a few important things to think about because it might take a lot longer than a buy and hold approach.

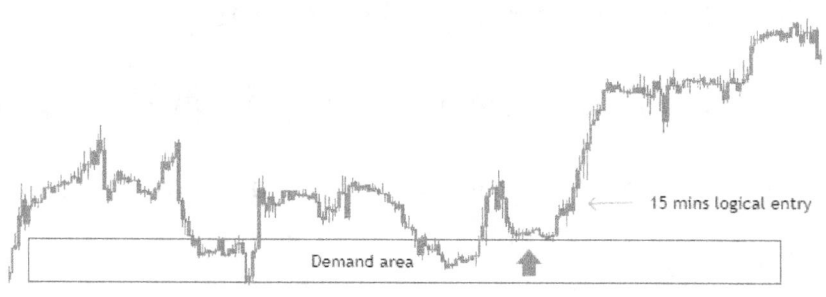

When investing, daily fluctuations have little bearing on the big picture because the emphasis is on longer-term market movements. On the other hand, the emphasis while day trading is on the variables that might influence intraday market movement. These consist of:

Liquidity

Measured by the ease with which a position may be bought or sold in the market, liquidity is a crucial component of trading, particularly day trading.

The speed at which an asset may be exchanged without changing its price is referred to as its liquidity, and it represents the condition of the market for that asset.

High liquidity markets are those for assets that may be sold fast with little to no effect on the asset's price; low liquidity is indicated by the opposite characteristics in a market.

Any asset that is exchanged in a market system, including cash, securities, real estate, and high-end goods, is covered by the idea of liquidity. The most illiquid asset class is thought to be uncommon luxury goods like wine and art, whereas cash is seen to be the most liquid.

For day traders, particularly those who make money by making several transactions, each for a tiny profit, liquidity is crucial.

For a traded security, a lack of liquidity can be the difference between hitting a profit objective and incurring a loss on an otherwise flawless deal. To determine a security's liquidity for the intended time period for trade execution, traders typically look to the daily or hourly volume traded for that asset.

It is important to take into account both the overall volume of securities exchanged and the order size for trade execution in relation to the average volume traded during that period.

Typically, day traders won't have many liquidity issues while placing trades in well-known stock, bonds, currencies, or commodities. Nevertheless, there are a lot more unusual and obscure securities with persistently low liquidity, meaning that even little order sizes can cause the market's price to fluctuate and cause traders to lose money on their holdings as they wait for their orders to clear.

How simple and quick it is to enter and exit a market is its liquidity. Because day traders are likely to execute many deals during the day, high liquidity is critical.

Understanding liquidity is crucial for traders since it affects transaction execution directly and contributes to the stability of today's financial markets on a bigger scale.

When asset values typically decline, the contagion that follows periods of usually low liquidity in the financial markets can present both great trading opportunities and the possibility of substantial losses.

However, as most day trading methods are centered on the capacity to join and exit positions quickly often even avoiding losses on unsuccessful trades by prompt position closing day traders typically steer clear of pairs with low levels of liquidity.

Before making a deal, day traders must be aware of the trading volume for a security and even monitor the typical volumes for the time of day they plan to execute their transaction.

Volatility

For day traders, the volatility of an asset that is, the speed at which the price fluctuates is crucial. If significant volatility is predicted during the day, there may be several possibilities for quick gains due to market moves.

Using a disciplined technique will help you learn how to regulate volatility to your advantage and lower risks.

Price change is a constant in financial markets. This is a good thing since it would make trading unprofitable if prices never changed.

Prices can change more quickly than they usually do. The degree or pace of price change (either way) is known as volatility. With volatility comes the potential for quick financial gain. As a trade-off, more volatility entails higher risk.

When volatility spikes, you may be able to achieve above-average returns, but you also run the risk of losing more money in a shorter period of time.

You may be able to take advantage of volatility and reduce your risks if you have discipline.

Before you attempt to trade in volatile markets, make sure you are prepared both psychologically and tactically to face the increased risks involved. This suggests

When there is a lot of volatility, you trade comfortably.

You are aware that there might be a significant financial loss.

If you're "ready for action," the next thing to do is make that your trading strategy's risk-control techniques are still being used.

Two significant factors are size of position and stop order placement. (Note: You may set price triggers for sales with a stop orders, which can help protect an unrealized gain or reduce potential losses on an existing position.) In volatile markets, some traders place their stop prices farther from the current market price than they would in calmer times and execute smaller deals, meaning they spend less cash in each trade.

The aim is to keep your overall risk exposure relatively constant while reducing the possibility that wider-than-normal intraday price swings may result in an early stop out. As always, bear in mind that in situations when there is a large price disparity or rapid market movement, stop orders may be executed considerably away from the stop price.

In volatile markets, profits can evaporate fast and turn into losses, so consider locking in more gains whenever possible. One tactic in this case could be to reduce the profit target for certain of your trades. As an alternative, you can decide to sell a portion of your stake and hang onto the remaining amount to benefit from any future rises if the value of the currency you sold is growing fast.

Volume of trades

The trade volume of an asset is a measurement of how frequently it is purchased or sold during a specific time frame. A large trade volume usually indicative of strong interest and may be used to determine when to enter and quit the market.

"Volume" in trading refers to the total number of units that can be exchanged during a certain time frame.

Because it informs them of an asset's liquidity level and how simple it is to enter or exit a position near the present price, traders depend on it as a critical statistic.

Using volume analysis, you may find the links between volume and pricing to predict the trades you will make. Purchasing volume and selling volume are the two main ideas of volume analysis.

When buyers are in control, purchase volume occurs at the offer price, which is the lowest price that sellers will accept on paper.

Sell volume occurs at the bid price, which is the highest price that buyers can offer, when sellers have greater influence.

A price chart's volume is usually shown by vertical bars at the bottom that show the number of shares that have changed hands over time.

Days with higher-than-normal volume typically see significant price fluctuations, which suggest something is off with the market.

Strategies for day trading forex

Since day trading merely requires you to close a deal before closing it overnight, it's more of a trading style than a technique in and of itself. Common techniques for day trading, whether on forex or another market, consist of:

- Trading trends
- swing trading
- scalping

Trading trends

By observing the movement of asset prices and making decisions about buying or selling based on the trend, trend traders try to earn money.

In the event that prices are rising and setting higher highs, traders would take a long position and purchase the asset. In the event that prices are trending lower and making a series of lower lows, traders would sell to take a short position.

Because trend trading allows you to hold onto your position for as long as the trend persists, it is not only a tool utilized by day traders. If you're going to remain with intraday trading, though, you would close it before the end of the day.

Trading swings

Taking advantage of short-term price patterns on the presumption that prices never move in a single direction throughout a trend is the essence of swing trading. Rather, swing traders aim to make money from both the upward and downward moves that take place over shorter periods of time.

Swing traders are typically more concerned in the slight reversals in a market's price movement than trend traders, who aim to profit from long-term market trends. They try to anticipate these reversals and trade in an effort to benefit from minute changes in the market.

Scalping

With an emphasis on attaining a high win rate, scalping is a short-term trading method that takes little but frequent profits. The idea is that collecting consistent little profits will help you amass a large trading account just as readily as making fewer deals and trying to lock in profits over time. Because losses might quickly offset gains, scaling calls for a highly tight exit plan.

Because overnight funding costs quickly erode the modest profit margins from each transaction, the majority of scalpers will exit positions before the end of the day.

Price Momentum

By assuming positions in financial instruments that show significant price swings, traders who employ the well-liked and extensively-used momentum trading method aim to profit from market trends.

This strategy is predicated on the idea that short- to medium-term price moves in a specific direction tend to persist.

One of the most basic types of trading is momentum trading, in which investors purchase and sell assets according to the strength of their recent price movement. According to theory, a price shift that is sufficiently driven in a particular direction is likely to persist for a while.

Volume day trading is preferred by traders since it makes it easier to enter and exit positions, no matter how big or little. The number of shares that are traded in investments on a typical day is shown by the average volume figure. There will be days when the volume is far lower than usual and days when it is substantially larger.

Keep an eye out for days when the volume is higher than normal. These are often days of great price fluctuation, either up or down. The price will drop if the majority of the volume is at the bid price, and the higher volume indicates that sellers are eager to part with their potions.

The market price will rise if the majority of the volume was transacted at the ask price due to demand and price availability.

The higher volume indicates that buyers are ready to enter a buy setup because they think the price is moving.

An increase in volume usually indicates a change in the market. Usually, volume trading is abruptly influenced by a news release or active traders who have been excited or nervous about the market prospects.

Thank you for purchasing this book.

GET INSTANT ACCESS TO THE FREE VIDEO COURSE BY FOLLOWING THE BELOW LINK

subscribepage.io/freeforexcourse

Click or copy and paste the above link on your browser for instant access to the bonus video.

Happy Trading!